Dear Barbara –

To a women that e very
much admire and love!

quilting

❑ ❑ ❑

poems 1987-1990

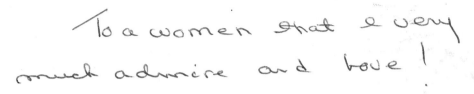

quilting

poems 1987-1990

by lucille clifton

BOA Editions Ltd. ❏ Brockport, New York ❏ 1991

Copyright © 1991 by Lucille Clifton
All rights reserved.

ISBN: 0-918526-80-9 cloth
ISBN: 0-918526-81-7 paper

LC #: 91-70845

First Edition

The publication of this book was made possible in part with the
assistance of a grant from the New York State Council on the Arts.

BOA Editions, Ltd. is a non-profit literary organization.

Designed and typeset by Visual Studies Workshop
Manufactured by McNaughton & Gunn, Lithographers

BOA Logo: Mirko

BOA Editions, Ltd.
A. Poulin, Jr., President
92 Park Avenue
Brockport, NY 14420

for maude meehan
homegirl

contents

[section titles are taken from
the names of traditional quilt designs]

eight-pointed star

tree of life

prayer

❏

❏

quilting

quilting

somewhere in the unknown world
a yellow eyed woman
sits with her daughter
quilting.

some other where
alchemists mumble over pots.
their chemistry stirs
into science. their science
freezes into stone.

in the unknown world
the woman
threading together her need
and her needle
nods toward the smiling girl
remember
this will keep us warm.

how does this poem end?
    do the daughters' daughters quilt?
    do the alchemists practice their tables?
    do the worlds continue spinning
    away from each other forever?

❏

log cabin

❏ ❏ ❏

i am accused of tending to the past
as if i made it,
as if i sculpted it
with my own hands. i did not.
this past was waiting for me
when i came,
a monstrous unnamed baby,
and i with my mother's itch
took it to breast
and named it
History.
she is more human now,
learning language everyday,
remembering faces, names and dates.
when she is strong enough to travel
on her own, beware, she will.

❏

note to my self

it's a black thing you wouldn't understand
                                        (t-shirt)

amira baraka—*i refuse to be judged by white men.*

or defined. and i see
that even the best believe
they have that right,
believe that
what they say i mean
is what i mean
as if words only matter in the world they know,
as if when i choose words
i must choose those
that they can live with
even if something inside me
cannot live,
as if my story is
so trivial
we can forget together,
as if i am not scarred,
as if my family enemy
does not look like them,
as if i have not reached
across our history to touch,
to soothe on more than one
occasion
and will again,
although the merely human
is denied me still
and i am now no longer beast
but saint.

❏

poem beginning in no and ending in yes

for hector peterson, aged 13
first child killed in soweto riot, 1976

no
light there was no light at first around the head
of the young boy   only the slim stirring of soweto
only the shadow of voices   students and soldiers
practicing their lessons   and one and one cannot be even
two in afrikaans   then before the final hush
in the schoolyard in soweto   there was the burning of his name
into the most amazing science   the most ancient prophesy
let there be light and there was light around the young
boy hector peterson dead in soweto and still among us
yes

❏

february 11, 1990

for Nelson Mandela and Winnie

nothing so certain as justice.
nothing so certain as time.
so he would wait seven days, or years
or twenty-seven even,
firm in his certainty .
nothing so patient as truth.
nothing so faithful as now.
walk out old chief, old husband,
enter again your own wife.

❏

at the cemetery,
walnut grove plantation, south carolina, 1989

among the rocks
at walnut grove
your silence drumming
in my bones,
tell me your names.

nobody mentioned slaves
and yet the curious tools
shine with your fingerprints.
nobody mentioned slaves
but somebody did this work
who had no guide, no stone,
who moulders under rock.

tell me your names,
tell me your bashful names
and i will testify.

the inventory lists ten slaves
but only men were recognized.

among the rocks
at walnut grove
some of these honored dead
were dark
some of these dark
were slaves
some of these slaves
were women
some of them did this
honored work.
tell me your names
foremothers, brothers,

tell me your dishonored names.
here lies
here lies
here lies
here lies
hear

❏

slave cabin,
sotterly plantation, maryland, 1989

in this little room
note carefully

aunt nanny's bench

three words that label
things
aunt
is my parent's sister
nanny
my grandmother
bench
the board at which
i stare
the soft curved polished
wood
that held her bottom
after the long days
without end
without beginning
when she   aunt nanny   sat
feet dead against the dirty floor
humming for herself   humming
her own sweet human name

❏

white lady

a street name for cocaine

wants my son
wants my niece
wants josie's daughter
holds them hard
and close as slavery
what will it cost
to keep our children
what will it cost
to buy them back.

white lady
says i want you
whispers
let me be your lover
whispers
run me through your
fingers
feel me smell me taste me
love me
nobody understands you like
white lady

white lady
you have chained our sons
in the basement
of the big house
white lady

you have walked our daughters
out into the streets
white lady
what do we have to pay
to repossess our children
white lady
what do we have to owe
to own our own at last

❏

memo

to fannie lou hamer

fannie for this
you never walked
miles through the mud
to register the vote
not for this
fannie did you stand
a wall in the hall
of justice not for these
stoned girls and boys
were you a brick
building a mississippi
building freedom
into a party not
this party fannie
where they lie eyes
cold and round as death
doing to us what even
slavery couldn't

❏

[from a letter written to Dr. W. E. B. Dubois by Alvin Borgquest
of Clark University in Massachusetts and dated April 3, 1905:

"We are pursuing an investigation here on the subject of
crying as an expression of the emotions, and should like
very much to learn about its peculiarities among the
colored people. We have been referred to you as a person
competent to give us information on the subject. We
desire especially to know about the following salient
aspects: 1. Whether the Negro sheds tears...."]

    reply

    he do
    she do
    they live
    they love
    they try
    they tire
    they flee
    they fight
    they bleed
    they break
    they moan
    they mourn
    they weep
    they die
    they do
    they do
    they do

❏

whose side are you on?

the side of the busstop woman
trying to drag her bag
up the front steps before the doors
clang shut   i am on her side
i give her exact change
and him the old man hanging by
one strap his work hand folded shut
as the bus doors i am on his side
when he needs to leave
i ring the bell i am on their side
riding the late bus into the same
someplace   i am on the dark side always
the side of my daughters
the side of my tired sons

❏

shooting star

who would i expect
to understand
what it be like
what it be like
living under a star
that hates you. you
spend a half life
looking for your own
particular heaven,
expecting to be found
one day on a sidewalk
in a bad neighborhood,
face toward the sky,
hoping some body saw
a blaze of light perhaps
a shooting star
some thing to make it mean
some thing.   yo,
that brilliance there,
is it you, huey?
is it huey?
is it you?

for huey p. newton
r.i.p.

❏

poem with rhyme in it

black people we live in the land
of ones who have cut off their own
two hands
and cannot pick up the strings
connecting them to their lives
who cannot touch   whose things
have turned into planets more dangerous
than mars
but i have listened this long dark night
to the stars
black people and though the ground
be bitter as salt
they say it is not our fault

❏

eyes

*for Clarence Fountain and the Five Blind Boys Of Alabama after
viewing* THE GOSPEL AT COLONUS, *the story of Oedipus
transplanted to a Southern Baptist Church, and thinking of my
grandfather and the history of my people on this land. Each section
opens with lyrics quoted from the musical.*

> "Here they are. The soft eyes open."
> —James Dickey

1.
*live where you can
be happy as you can
happier than god has made your father*

wandering colonus
as you have wandered selma
and montgomery
as you have circuited
the southern church halls
half-emptied by a young war
wandered from your mothers
then seeking them again   again
the dim remembered breasts
offered without judgement
live
you sing to us
live where you can

2.
where have we come to now
what ground is this
what god is honored here

the fields of alabama sparkle in the sun   on
broadway
five old men
sparkle in white suits
their fingers light
on one another's back   lights
proclaim The Five Blind Boys
Of Alabama   five old men
black and blind
who have no names save one
what ground is this
what god

3.
i could say much to you
if you could understand me

the gods announce themselves to men
by name   clarence fountain's hand
pushes aside the air
between himself and vision
vision of resting place
of sanctuary
clarence fountain's hand
commands the air
he has seen what he has seen
it has been enough

4.
a voice foretold
that i shall find
sanctuary

somewhere in alabama
a baby is born to a girl
in a tarpaper room
his blind hand shivers
groping toward her breasts
as toward a lamp
she holds him to her
and begins to sing
live where you can
be happy as you can
slowly
the soft eyes open

5.
all eyes fail
before time's eye

it has been enough
slowly the soft eyes open
what ground is this
what god
i could say much to you
be happy as you can

❏

defending my tongue

what i be talking about
can be said in this language
only   this tongue
be the one that understands
what i be talking about

you are you talking about
the landscape that would break me
if it could   the trees
my grandfolk swung from   the dirt
they planted in and ate

no what i be talking about
the dirt   the tree   the land
scape can only be said
in this language   the words
be hard be bumping out too much
to be contained in one thin tongue
like this language   this landscape   this life

❏

catalpa flower

❏   ❏   ❏

from the wisdom of sister brown

1.
on sisterhood

some of our sisters
who put down the bucket
lookin for us
to pick it up

2.
on lena (born 6/30/17)

people talk about beautiful
and look at lizabeth taylor
lena just stand there smilin
a tricky smile

3.
on the difference between
eddie murphy and richard pryor

eddie, he a young blood
he see somethin funny
in everythin   ol rich
been around a long time
he know aint nothin
really funny

❏

the birth of language

and adam rose
fearful in the garden
without words
for the grass
his fingers plucked
without a tongue
to name the taste
shimmering in his mouth
did they draw blood
the blades   did it become
his early lunge
toward language
did his astonishment
surround him
did he shudder
did he whisper
eve

❏

we are running

running and
time is clocking us
from the edge like an only
daughter.
our mothers stream before us,
cradling their breasts in their
hands.
oh pray that what we want
is worth this running,
pray that what we're running
toward
is what we want.

❏

what the grass knew

after some days, toward evening,
He stood under a brackish sky
trembling and blaming creation.
but the grass knew that what is built
is finally built for others,
that firmament is not enough, that
tiger was coming and partridge and
whale and even their raucous voices
would not satisfy. He, walking
the cool of the garden, lonely
as light, realized that He must feed
His own hunger or die. adam,
He nodded, adam,
while the understanding grass
prepared itself for eve.

❑

nude photograph

here is the woman's
soft and vulnerable body,
every where on her turning
round into another
where. shadows on her
promising mysterious places
promising the answers to
questions impossible to ask.
who could rest one hand here or here
and not feel, whatever the shape
of the great hump longed for
in the night, a certain joy, a certain,
yes, satisfaction, yes.

❏

this is for the mice that live
behind the baseboard,
she whispered, her fingers
thick with cheese. what i do
is call them, copying their own
voices; please please please
sweet please. i promise
them nothing. they come
bringing nothing and we sit
together, nuzzling each other's
hungry hands. everything i want
i have to ask for, she sighed.

❏

sleeping beauty

when she woke up
she was terrible.
under his mouth her mouth
turned red and warm
then almost crimson as the coals
smothered and forgotten
in the grate.
she had been gone so long.
there was so much to unlearn.
she opened her eyes.
he was the first thing she saw
and she blamed him.

❏

a woman who loves
impossible men
sits a long time indoors
watching her windows
she has no brother
who understands
where she is not going
her sisters offer their
own breasts up, full and
creamy vessels but she
cannot drink because
she loves impossible men

a woman who loves
impossible men
listens at night to music
she cannot sing
she drinks good sherry
swallowing around the notes
rusted in her throat
but she does not fill
she is already full
of love for impossible men

a woman who loves
impossible men
promises each morning
that she will take this day in her
hands
disrobe it   lie with it
learn to love it
but she doesn't   she walks by
strangers   walks by kin
forgets their birthmarks
their birthdays
remembers only the names
the stains of impossible men

❏

man and wife

she blames him, at the last, for
backing away from his bones
and his woman, from the life
he promised her was worth
cold sheets. she blames him
for being unable to see
the tears in her eyes, the birds
hovered by the window, for love being
not enough, for leaving.

he blames her, at the last, for
holding him back with her eyes
beyond when the pain was more
than he was prepared to bear,
for the tears he could neither
end nor ignore, for believing
that love could be enough,
for the birds, for the life
so difficult to leave.

❑

poem in praise of menstruation

if there is a river
more beautiful than this
bright as the blood
red edge of the moon   if

there is a river
more faithful than this
returning each month
to the same delta   if there

is a river
braver than this
coming and coming in a surge
of passion, of pain   if there is

a river
more ancient than this
daughter of eve
mother of cain and of abel   if there is in

the universe such a river   if
there is some where water
more powerful than this wild
water
pray that it flows also
through animals
beautiful and faithful and ancient
and female and brave

❏

peeping tom

sometimes at night he dreams back
thirty years
to the alley outside our room
where he stands, a tiptoed boy
watching the marvelous thing
a man turning into a woman.
sometimes
beating himself with his own fist
into that spilled boy and the
imagined world of that man
that woman that night, he lies
turned from his natural wife.
sometimes he searches the window for
a plaid cap, two wide eyes.

❏

ways you are not like oedipus

for Michael Glaser

you have spared your father
you pass the sphinx without
answering   you recognized
your mother in time
your sons covet only
their own kingdoms
you lead your daughters
even in your blindness
you do not wander far
from your own good house
it is home and you know it

❏

the killing of the trees

the third went down
with a sound almost like flaking,
a soft swish as the left leaves
fluttered themselves and died.
three of them, four, then five
stiffening in the snow
as if this hill were Wounded Knee
as if the slim feathered branches
were bonnets of war
as if the pale man seated
high in the bulldozer nest
his blonde mustache ice-matted
was Pahuska come again but stronger now,
his long hair wild and unrelenting.

remember the photograph,
the old warrior, his stiffened arm
raised as if in blessing,
his frozen eyes open,
his bark skin brown and not so much
wrinkled as circled with age,
and the snow everywhere still falling,
covering his one good leg.
remember his name was Spotted Tail
or Hump or Red Cloud or Geronimo
or none of these or all of these.
he was a chief. he was a tree
falling the way a chief falls,
straight, eyes open, arms reaching
for his mother ground.

so i have come to live
among the men who kill the trees,
a subdivision, new,

in southern Maryland.
I have brought my witness eye with me
and my two wild hands,
the left one sister to the fists
pushing the bulldozer against the old oak,
the angry right, brown and hard and spotted
as bark. we come in peace,
but this morning
ponies circle what is left of life
and whales and continents and children and ozone
and trees huddle in a camp weeping
outside my window and i can see it all
with that one good eye.

❏

pahuska=long hair, lakota name for custer

questions and answers

what must it be like
to stand so firm, so sure?

in the desert even the saguro
hold on as long as they can

twisting their arms in
protest or celebration.

you are like me,
understanding the surprise

of jesus, his rough feet
planted on the water

the water lapping
his toes and holding them.

you are like me, like him
perhaps, certain only that

the surest failure
is the unattempted walk.

❏

november 21, 1988

25 years

those days
before the brain blew back
mottled and rusting against the pink coat
them days
when the word had meaning
as well as definition
those days
when honor was honorable and
good and right were good and right
them days
when the spirit of hope
reached toward us waving a wide hand
and smiling toward us   yes
those days
them days
the days
before the bubble closed
over the top of the world   no
this is not better than that

❏

the beginning of the end of the world

cockroach population possibly declining
—news report

maybe the morning the roaches
walked into the kitchen
bold with they bad selves
marching up out of the drains
not like soldiers   like priests
grim and patient in the sink
and when we ran the water
trying to drown them as if they were
soldiers   they seemed to bow their
sad heads   for us not at us
and march single file away

maybe then   the morning we rose
from our beds as always
listening for the bang of the end
of the world   maybe then
when we heard only the tiny tapping
and saw them dark and prayerful
in the kitchen   maybe then
when we watched them turn from us
faithless at last
and walk in a long line away

❏

the last day

we will find ourselves surrounded
by our kind   all of them now
wearing the eyes they had
only imagined possible
and they will reproach us
with those eyes
in a language more actual
than speech
asking why we allowed this
to happen   asking why
for the love of God
we did this to ourselves
and we will answer
in our feeble voices   because
because   because

❏

eight-pointed star

❑   ❑   ❑

wild blessings

licked in the palm of my hand
by an uninvited woman. so i have held
in that hand the hand of a man who
emptied into his daughter, the hand
of a girl who threw herself
from a tenement window, the trembling
junkie hand of a priest, of a boy who
shattered across viet nam
someone resembling his mother,
and more. and more.
do not ask me to thank the tongue
that circled my fingers
or pride myself on the attentions
of the holy lost.
i am grateful for many blessings
but the gift of understanding,
the wild one, maybe not.

❏

somewhere
some woman
just like me
tests the lock on the window
in the children's room,
lays out tomorrow's school clothes,
sets the table for breakfast early,
finds a pen between the cushions
on the couch
sits down and writes the words
Good Times.
i think of her as i begin to teach
the lives of the poets,
about her space at the table
and my own inexplicable life.

❏

1

when i stand around among poets
i am embarrassed mostly,
their long white heads,
the great bulge in their pants,

their certainties.

i don't know how to do
what i do in the way
that i do it. it happens
despite me and i pretend

to deserve it.

but i don't know how to do it.
only sometimes when
something is singing
i listen and so far

i hear.

2

when i stand around
among poets, sometimes
i hear a single music
in us, one note
dancing us through the
singular moving world.

❏

water sign woman

the woman who feels everything
sits in her new house
waiting for someone to come
who knows how to carry water
without spilling, who knows
why the desert is sprinkled
with salt, why tomorrow
is such a long and ominous word.

they say to the feel things woman
that little she dreams is possible,
that there is only so much
joy to go around, only so much
water. there are no questions
for this, no arguments. she has

to forget to remember the edge
of the sea, they say, to forget
how to swim to the edge, she has
to forget how to feel. the woman
who feels everything sits in her
new house retaining the secret
the desert knew when it walked
up from the ocean, the desert,

so beautiful in her eyes;
water will come again
if you can wait for it.
she feels what the desert feels.
she waits.

❏

photograph

my grandsons
spinning in their joy

universe
keep them turning   turning
black blurs against the window
of the world
for they are beautiful
and there is trouble coming
round and round and round

❏

grandma, we are poets

autism: from Webster's New Universal Dictionary
and the Random House Encyclopedia

in psychology a state of mind
characterized by daydreaming

say rather
i imagined myself
in the place before
language imprisoned itself
in words

by failure to use language normally

say rather that labels
and names rearranged themselves
into description
so that what i saw
i wanted to say

by hallucinations, and ritualistic and repetitive
patterns of behavior
such as excessive rocking and spinning

say rather circling and
circling my mind i am sure i imagined
children without small rooms
imagined young men black and
filled with holes imagined
girls imagined old men penned
imagined actual humans
howling their animal fear

by failure to relate to others

say rather they began
to recede to run back
ward as it were
into a world of words
apartheid   hunger   war
i could not follow

by disregard of external reality,
withdrawing into a private world

say rather i withdrew
to seek within myself
some small reassurance
that tragedy while vast
is bearable

❏

december 7, 1989

this morning your grandmother
sits in the shadow of
Pearl drinking her coffee.
a sneak attack would find me
where my mother sat that day,
flush against her kitchen table,
her big breasts leaning into
the sugar spill. and it is sweet
to be here in the space between
one horror and another
thinking that history
happens all the time
but is remembered backward
in labels not paragraphs.
and so i claim this day
and offer it
this paragraph i own
to you, peyo, dakotah,
for when you need some
memory, some honey thing
to taste, and call the past.

❏

to my friend, jerina

listen,
when i found there was no safety
in my father's house
i knew there was none anywhere.
you are right about this,
how i nurtured my work
not my self, how i left the girl
wallowing in her own shame
and took on the flesh of my mother.
but listen,
the girl is rising in me,
not willing to be left to
the silent fingers in the dark,
and you are right,
she is asking for more than
most men are able to give,
but she means to have what she
has earned,
sweet sighs, safe houses,
hands she can trust.

❏

lot's wife   1988

each of these weeds is a day
i climbed the stair
at 254 purdy street
and looked into a mirror
to see if i was really there.
i was there.   i am there
in the thousand days.
the weeds.   and these weeds

were 11 harwood place
that daddy bought expecting it
to hold our name forever
against the spin of the world.

our name is spinning away in the wind
blowing across the vacant lots
of buffalo, new york,
that were my girlhood homes.

sayles, i hear them calling, sayles,
we thought we would live forever;
and i look back like lot's wife
wedded to her weeds and turn to something
surer than salt and write this, yes
i promise, yes we will.

❏

**fat fat
water rat**

imagine the children singing
to a thin woman. imagine
her tight lips, the shadow
and bone of her ass
as she enters this room
and you see her and whisper,
beautiful.

imagine she is myself,
next year perhaps, passing
the now silent children,
entering this room and you,
not recognizing the water rat,
feel your tongue thickening,
everything thickening.

in my dream i swim away from her
as often as toward. in my dream
the children are singing
or silent, it never matters,
and i am of uncertain size
and shape, lying splendid in
a giant's bed. imagine this room
and me spreading for you my thighs,
my other beautiful things.

❏

poem to my uterus

you   uterus
you have been patient
as a sock
while i have slippered into you
my dead and living children
now
they want to cut you out
stocking i will not need
where i am going
where am i going
old girl
without you
uterus
my bloody print
my estrogen kitchen
my black bag of desire
where can i go
barefoot
without you
where can you go
without me

❏

to my last period

well girl, goodbye,
after thirty-eight years.
thirty-eight years and you
never arrived
splendid in your red dress
without trouble for me
somewhere, somehow.

now it is done,
and i feel just like
the grandmothers who,
after the hussy has gone,
sit holding her photograph
and sighing, *wasn't she*
beautiful? wasn't she beautiful?

❑

wishes for sons

i wish them cramps.
i wish them a strange town
and the last tampon.
i wish them no 7-11.

i wish them one week early
and wearing a white skirt.
i wish them one week late.

later i wish them hot flashes
and clots like you
wouldn't believe.   let the
flashes come when they
meet someone special.
let the clots come
when they want to.

let them think they have accepted
arrogance in the universe,
then bring them to gynecologists
not unlike themselves.

❏

the mother's story

a line of women i don't know,
she said,
came in and whispered over you
each one fierce word,
she said, each word
more powerful than one before.
and i thought what is this to bring
to one black girl from buffalo
until the last one came and smiled,
she said,
and filled your ear with light
and that, she said, has been the one,
the last one, that last one.

❏

in which i consider the fortunate deaf

the language palpable,
their palm prints folded around
the names of the things.
seasons like skin
snuggled against fingerbone
and their wonder at loving
someone like you perhaps,
even your absence tangible,
your cold name fastened
into their shivering hands.

❏

4/25/89   late

(f. diagnosed w. cancer 4/25/84)

when i awake
the time will have jerked back
into five years ago,
the sea will not be this one,
you will run
under a grayer sky
wearing that green knit cap
we laughed about
and, sweating home again
after your run, all fit
and well and safe, you will
prepare to meet that
stethescopic group
and hear yourself pronounced
an almost ghost.

❏

as he was dying
a canticle of birds
hovered
watching through the glass
as if to catch
that final breath
and sing it   where?
he died.
there was a shattering of wing
that sounded   then did not sound,
and we stood in this silence
blackly   some would say,
while through the windows,
as perhaps at other times,
the birds, if they had stayed,
could see us,
and i do not mean white here,
but as we are,
transparent women and transparent men.

❏

night sound

the sound of a woman breathing
who has inhaled already
past her mother, who has left
behind more days than are ahead,
who must measure her exhalations
carefully, who spends these cries,
these soft expensive murmurings on you

man   breathing as if there could be
a surplus of air, of evening,
as if there could be even now
no question of tomorrow.

❏

the spirit walks in
through the door
of the flesh's house

the rooms leading off
from the hall
burn with color

the spirit feels
the door behind her close

and the sinister hall
is thick with the one word
Choose

the poet walks
in through the door
of the scholar's house

the rooms leading off
from the hall
buzz with language

the poet
feels the door
behind her close

and the sinister hall
is dark with the one word
Choose

❏

after the reading

tired from being a poet
i throw myself onto
Howard Johnson's bed
and long for home,
that sad mysterious country
where nobody notices
a word i say, nobody
thinks more of me or less
than they would think of any
chattering thing; mice
running toward the dark, leaves
rubbing against one another,
words tumbling together
up the long stair, home,
my own cheap lamp i can switch off
pretending i'm at peace there
in the dark. home. i sink at last into
the poet's short and fitful sleep.

❏

moonchild

only after the death
of the man who killed the bear,
after the death of the coalminer's son,
did i remember that the moon
also rises, coming heavy or thin
over the living fields, over
the cities of the dead;
only then did i remember how she
catches the sun and keeps most of him
for the evening that surely will come;
and it comes.
only then did i know that to live
in the world all that i needed was
some small light and know that indeed
i would rise again and rise again to dance.

❏

tree of life

❏ ❏ ❏

How art thou fallen from Heaven,
O Lucifer, son of the morning?...
—Isaiah 14: 12

oh where have you fallen to
son of the morning
beautiful lucifer
bringer of light
it is all shadow
in heaven without you
the cherubim sing
kaddish

    and even the
solitary brother
has risen from his seat
of stones   he is holding
they say   a wooden stick
and pointing toward
a garden

    light breaks
where no light was before
where no eye is prepared
to see
and animals rise up to walk
oh lucifer
what have you done

❏

remembering the birth of lucifer

some will remember
the flash of light
as he broke
from the littlest finger
of God   some will
recall the bright shimmer
and then
flush in the tremble of air
so much shine

even then   the seraphim say
they knew
it was too much for
one small heaven
they rustled their three wings
they say   and began
to wait   and to watch

❏

whispered to lucifer

lucifer six-finger
where have you gone to
with your swift lightning

oh son of the morning
was it the woman
enticed you to leave us

was it to touch her
featherless arm
was it to curl your belly

around her
that you fell laughing
your grace all ashard

leaving us here in
perpetual evening
even the guardians

silent   all of us
going about our
father's business

less radiant
less sure

❏

eve's version

smooth talker
slides into my dreams
and fills them with apple
apple snug as my breast
in the palm of my hand
apple sleek apple sweet
and bright in my mouth

it is your own lush self
you hunger for
he whispers   lucifer
honey-tongue.

❏

lucifer understanding at last

thy servant lord

bearer of lightning
and of lust

thrust between the
legs of the earth
into this garden

phallus and father
doing holy work

oh sweet delight
oh eden

if the angels
hear of this

there will be no peace
in heaven

❏

the garden of delight

for some
it is stone
bare smooth
as a buttock
rounding
into the crevasse
of the world

for some
it is extravagant
water   mouths wide
washing together
forever   for some
it is fire
for some air

and for some
certain only of the syllables
it is the element they
search their lives for

eden

for them
it is a test

❏

adam thinking

she
stolen from my bone
is it any wonder
i hunger to tunnel back
inside   desperate
to reconnect the rib and clay
and to be whole again

some need is in me
struggling to roar through my
mouth into a name
this creation is so fierce
i would rather have been born

❏

eve thinking

it is wild country here
brothers and sisters coupling
claw and wing
groping one another

i wait
while the clay two-foot
rumbles in his chest
searching for language to

call me
but he is slow
tonight as he sleeps
i will whisper into his mouth
our names

❏

the story thus far

so they went out
clay and morning star
following the bright back
of the woman

as she walked past
the cherubim
turning their fiery swords
past the winged gate

into the unborn world
chaos fell away
before her like a cloud
and everywhere seemed light

seemed glorious
seemed very eden

❏

lucifer speaks in his own voice

sure as i am
of the seraphim
folding wing
so am i certain of a
graceful bed
and a soft caress
along my long belly
at endtime   it was
to be
i who was called son
if only of the morning
saw that some must
walk or all will crawl
so slithered into earth
and seized the serpent in
the animals   i became
the lord of snake for
adam and for eve
i   the only lucifer
light-bringer
created out of fire
illuminate i could
and so
illuminate i did

❏

prayer

❏ ❏ ❏

blessing the boats

(at St. Mary's)

may the tide
that is entering even now
the lip of our understanding
carry you out
beyond the face of fear
may you kiss
the wind then turn from it
certain that it will
love your back   may you
open your eyes to water
water waving forever
and may you in your innocence
sail through this to that

❏

acknowledgments

Grateful acknowledgment is made to the editors of the following journals and other publications in which some of the poems in this book (or earlier versions of them) were first published:

American Poetry Review: "oh where have you fallen to....,"
"remembering the birth of lucifer," "whispered to lucifer,"
"eve's version," "lucifer understanding at last," "the garden of delight," "adam thinking," "eve thinking," "the story thus far" and "lucifer speaks in his own voice";
Callaloo: "eyes";
Chelsea: "february 11, 1990," "to my friend, jerina" and "white lady";
George Washington University Review: "killing the trees";
MS: "wishes for sons";
Passager: "man & wife" and "night sounds";
Rhetoric Review: "grandma, we are poets";
River Styx: "poem in praise of menstruation" and "shooting star";
Zyzzyva: "poem beginning in no and ending in yes" and "peeping tom".

The italicized lines in the poem "eyes" are from *The Gospel at Colonnus,* adaptation by Lee Breuer. Copyright © 1989. Published by and reprinted with the permission of Theatre Communications Group, New York.

lucille clifton

Lucille Clifton was born in 1936 in Depew, New York, and educated at Howard University and the State University of New York at Fredonia.

Lucille Clifton's books of poetry include *Good Times* (1969), *Good News about the Earth* (1972), *An Ordinary Woman* (1974), *Two-Headed Woman* (1976), *Good Woman: Poems and a Memoir 1969-1980* and *Next: New Poems* (both published simultaneously by BOA Editions, Ltd. in 1987) and *Quilting: Poems 1987-1990* (1991). She is also the author of a memoir, *Generations* (1976), and of more than a dozen books of fiction and poetry for children.

Clifton's awards and distinctions as a poet and fiction writer include the University of Massachusetts Press's Juniper Prize for Poetry, a nomination for the Pulitzer Prize for Poetry for *Two-Headed Woman* and a second nomination for the Pulitzer Prize for both *Good Woman: Poems and a Memoir 1969-1980* and *Next: New Poems*, an Emmy Award from the American Academy of Television Arts and Sciences, creative writing fellowships from the National Endowment for the Arts, and Poet Laureate of the State of Maryland.

She has taught at Coppin State College, Goucher College, the American University in Washington, D. C., and the University of California at Santa Cruz. Her other teaching experiences have included appointments as Elliston Poet at the University of Cincinnati, Jenny Moore Lecturer in Creative Writing at George Washington University, and Woodrow Wilson Scholar at Fisk University, Trinity College, and other universities. She currently is Distinguished Professor of Humanities at St. Mary's College in Maryland.

❑

BOA Editions Ltd. American Poets Continuum Series

Vol. 1 *The Führer Bunker: A Cycle of Poems in Progress*
        W. D. Snodgrass
Vol. 2 *She*
        M. L. Rosenthal
Vol. 3 *Living with Distance*
        Ralph J. Mills, Jr.
Vol. 4 *Not Just Any Death*
        Michael Waters
Vol. 5 *That Was Then: New and Selected Poems*
        Isabella Gardner
Vol. 6 *Things That Happen Where There Aren't Any People*
        William Stafford
Vol. 7 *The Bridge of Change: Poems 1974-1980*
        John Logan
Vol. 8 *Signatures*
        Joseph Stroud
Vol. 9 *People Live Here: Selected Poems 1949-1983*
        Louis Simpson
Vol. 10 *Yin*
        Carolyn Kizer
Vol. 11 *Duhamel: Ideas of Order in Little Canada*
        Bill Tremblay
Vol. 12 *Seeing It Was So*
        Anthony Piccione
Vol. 13 *Hyam Plutzik: The Collected Poems*
Vol. 14 *Good Woman: Poems and a Memoir 1965-1980*
        Lucille Clifton
Vol. 15 *Next: New Poems*
        Lucille Clifton
Vol. 16 *Roxa: Voices of the Culver Family*
        William B. Patrick
Vol. 17 *John Logan: The Collected Poems*
Vol. 18 *Isabella Gardner: The Collected Poems*
Vol. 19 *The Sunken Lightship*
        Peter Makuck
Vol. 20 *The City in Which I Love You*
        Li-Young Lee
Vol. 21 *Quilting: Poems 1987-1990*
        Lucille Clifton